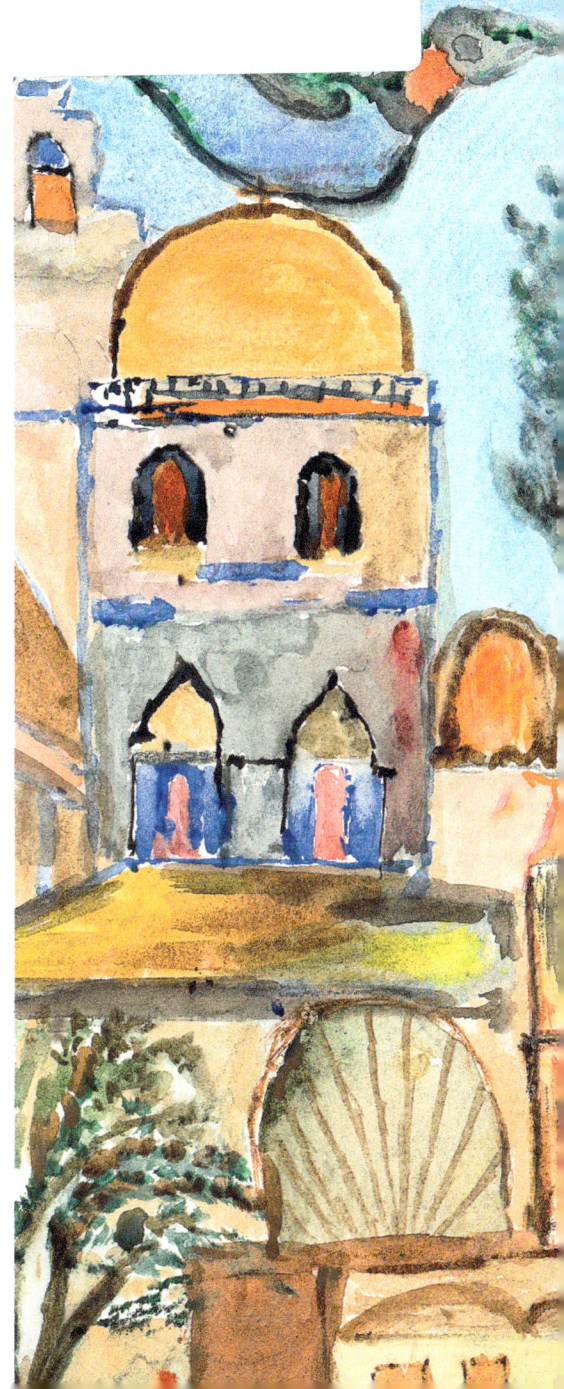

To Palestine with Love...

NAJWA KAWAR FARAH

RIMAL BOOKS

First published 2009

Second print 2024

Rimal Books, Cyprus

www.rimalbooks.com

ISBN 978-9963-610-37-2

Printed and bound in the UK.

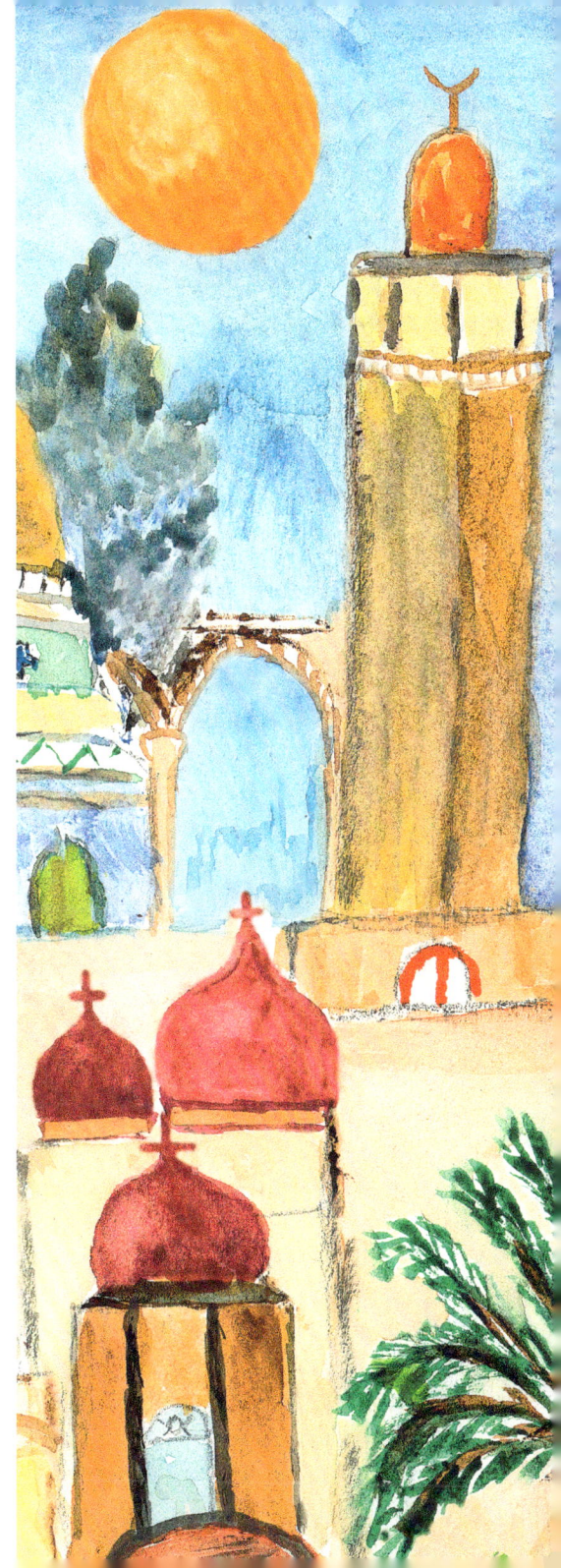

This Book is dedicated to the children of Palestine

'But so did he love his Palestine that he laid his life for it'

'The Giant' by Najwa Kawar Farah

Contents

Foreword

These poems were never intended for publication; they are expressions of inner feelings and impressions to which I resorted to explore and analyse in words the profundity of my soul. Whilst it is difficult to be objective about myself, my reaction to situations and places seems to be affected mainly by the impressions they leave on me rather than the practical considerations of life.

Nature, and woodlands especially, mean a lot to me. Traffic and city lights are a blur, but the shape and colour of every tree on the roadside are embedded in my memory, as much as the beauty of lonely mountain summits and the unlimited horizon of the plains are.

The injustice inflicted on my homeland, Palestine, made me profoundly angry and frustrated; how vulnerable we were under a British Mandate which dispossessed and waived the rights of its inhabitants. The Palestinian tragedy is a very personal matter for me, as it is for every Palestinian who is its victim in one way or the other.

Al-Andalus, the Spain of today, is not only a parallel for my world but a paradise lost, a near utopia where beauty in architecture, gardens, poetry, and music, as well as advancement in the sciences, medicine, and philosophy, reached their zenith and influenced the Renaissance in Europe. Although I never thought of myself as an artist, the paintings in this book are an expression of a passion to remember and bring back images of my country, its skylines, landscapes, flowers, trees, and to add zest and warmth to my life.

I am especially delighted with the fusion of word and picture that my granddaughter, Jumana, has captured in this compilation; a vital part of the continuation of the creative process is to touch, provoke, persuade, and influence; the whole is truly greater than the sum of the parts. My gratitude goes to my son Amin who helped in the translation from the Arabic originals and in guiding me to communicate better the meaning behind the words.

Finally to all those who suffer injustice, may meagre words inspire the downtrodden and humble the haughty; may splashes of colour lift the spirit of those who suffer and brighten the soul of the oppressor.

One Sunday in Jerusalem

Why is it after so many years
Many eventful years
That one day is singled out?
For nothing happened then.

It was Sunday afternoon,
A wind blew
And the beloved trees of Jerusalem
Swayed and bent,
Their dark foliage engulfed me with mysterious joy;
Ancient trees, standing there years
By a hospital, an embassy, a church, a mosque.
Something about them was deeply profound.

Many winds had visited those trees,
Those Jerusalem trees.
Did the winds tell about their birthplace, their journeys
Over rocky mountains and deep scented valleys?
Yet, this is where they want to linger,
To rest and belong.
And why, after so many years,
Does my soul journey to that Sunday in Jerusalem,
And why do memories, so vivid, so inexplicable,
Overwhelm me?
Is this eternity unravelled?
Is this where our spirit resides?

The Wind

On this day, what is the wind saying?
In this place, what secrets does it impart,
As it moves trees to mourn and invoke memories?

I stand here in surreal reality, rooted with
An overwhelming desire to be unified,
Embraced by the boughs of the trees
Soothed by the whispering warm wind,
As sunset exudes hues of evening enchantment.

To end this beginning is a crushing desire.
For this sad continuous change is heart-rending;
This compulsory parting from dear moments,
Acutely conscious of time's infinite march,
Points to the futility of our human endeavour.

Saffiyah

A jasmine pot alone, intoxicating on a window sill;
Its scent spreads, intruding Saffiyah's snatched daydream,
Into a room, under a roof of rusty tin sheets, a sprawl
Of ironmongery in Beirut's unhappy southern suburbs;
Home to the refugees of Palestine; a home of sufferance.

Her beloved is defending families and fending off foes.
Proud of him, she recalls his face and valiant deeds,
His handsome rugged face, strong arms, clenched fist.
Destroyer of tanks, fighter at the battle of Shaqeef castle;[1]
To him she must now make haste with nourishment.

With compatriot womenfolk, she busies herself at stove and sink;
The urgent need is a meal for fighters to share.
Around her the din of war, shouts and rush of men at arms;
She scurries, carrying oven fresh bread to his flimsy hideout,
The aromas of jasmine and hot bread clash in the dank alley.

The chatter of machine guns, silence, a crescendo of explosions.
He watches. She's frozen, framed against the alley wall.
Time flashes in slow motion; light, sound, heat, and burning flesh
Entwine into eternity, and hazy emptiness greets burning eyes;
Leaden legs kneel where a dismembered smouldering body lies still.

Alone he cries, kissing what was a cheek, a hand, a remnant;
The scent of jasmine spreads from a fallen broken pot;
Indifferent it lies on the blooded ground, as cats step nervously around;
In the dimming evening, facing the macabre scene, he sprinkles jasmine buds
On the sorry seared flesh of his beloved Saffiyah, now no more.

The heavens light up, and yet it is not Christmas Eve; phosphorous
Red, orange baubles of death dangle, and slowly fall from the sky.
Farewell, Saffiyah. Farewell snatches of shattered daydreams;
It seems like Christmas Eve; a Christmas Eve of gifts
To the children of Palestine.

[1]Crusader Castle

A Poet who loved the Poor

Grief has gnawed and eaten at your heart;
No solace comes from the nocturnal gardens of sorrow,
Whilst the sailing moon an argent sympathizer,
In circles still roams looking for a collaborator,
A messenger, who would deliver the message;
The night, as well, had become an ally,
Responding to your anguished questioning,

A witness to crimes committed behind its curtain of black
In the camps where Palestinians live their bondage,
Where blood and suffering reign;
Also in the quarters of Suallam and Leilaki,
And the squares of a city that was fair and joyful; for the
Dreams of the defeated are trampled by the stealthy steps of death.

Will your fascination with love, beauty, and truth ever be exhausted?
Oh my poet, anguish shall reveal your secret, as will
Your unanswered question will still reverberate and echo;
Will the rising generations stand up for the poor,
As you in your short life have done, dying for the cause?
For you, a wreath of roses I will place, where you lie under an oak tree
Rooted in a country that embraces the sun and caresses the moon.

The Wall

Winding through vale and plain this wall of hate and cement mix
Spits venom on land's long-rooted now muted guardian peoples.
Separate now is mother from child, and peasant from his olive grove.
Segregated is child from school bench, and faithful from their Sanctus.
What irony that you should rise where Christ, through love,
demolished mankind's walls.

The Church of the Resurrection beckons in vain
Its indigenous worshippers to return, repair, redeem, restore, and repent.
Faces pressed against callous concrete, they wait to enter its blessed gates
In a world seemingly oblivious of its treacherous bends.
Complicit in silence are the 'well meaning' with its constructor's scheme.

Oh little town of Bethlehem, where angels sang peace on earth and
goodwill to all men, concrete is your pain.
All men abandoned, desolate mothers; destitute children; devastated land
In the lap of Shepherds' Field no trace of fragile
Angels' wings is left nor echoes of heavenly choirs.
Complicit in silence are the 'well meaning' with its constructor's scheme.

Defying the scheming usurper the majestic
Dome of the Rock still steals the scene.
Its call to prayer heard falling on yearning souls.
Worshippers stand outside the gates, denied entry to its welcoming
hallowed grounds.
Complicit in silence are the 'well meaning' with its
constructor's scheme.

Yet in the field of all possibilities, uprooted lie one
Thousand trees aged for a thousand years;
Wise old branches survey
The garish grey wall to the East. It was built
To shut out shunned neighbours, but now it has the oppressor
Hemmed in by the sea;

In the field of all possibilities lies a cult of love where the rising sun
Banishes the dark divide between peoples
And the future is bright
When to their land Palestinians return and the blessed soil
Heaves a contented sigh as peace and justice prevail.

Siege

Another new day, another new strangle hold;
Beirut, bride of the Mediterranean, under siege;
Beirut, oasis of liberty, how I loved the freedom,
The poetry, the new horizons, the 'joie-de-vivre';
Beirut, city of learning, how I loved your intellect,
Loved a spirit ancient that abides in you;
A golden leap of joy, a dancing soul,
Poetry, fruits of the mind and beauty;
How much I loved you, Beirut.

But alas again, here we are both besieged;
Planes swoop from the skies sowing seeds
Of death and destruction, as your delicate
Fabric absorbs phosphorus, cluster, and
Vacuum explosions of annihilation, seeking
Your burdened Palestinian uninvited guests

So does it matter Beirut, this siege?
Isn't this another wall encircling other walls?
Are there seven or more?

No trumpet by an invader need make them fall;
For my soul is incarcerated in depression
As in this concentration camp we seek existence,
And in this desert of emptiness
We ask, have men lost their reason,
Or is justice yet another myth?

But, Beirut, there are moments
Of illumination, of revelation,
When your fragrance spreads,
When memory is kind,
When the curtains of depression lift;
And I remember the hills of Nazareth,
Flickering lights in the villages of Jerusalem,
And those who stand fast in my country
Until Jerusalem days come back.
Then! Then the suffering of my people will cease.
Then, my soul that is bent within me
For a moment will find solace, even joy.

Autumn Leaves

Hues of red carpet the park where autumn leaves trembling lie;
Now playful November winds tease and chase them away;
Nervous and flustered, they twirl, settle, and then are gusted away.
Like golden winged birds, they swoop and dart, driven by the wind;
Fleeing the comfort of the forest floor, are they seeking to end it all?
A fluttering flashing display; chaffing shooing sounds of silence;
Sweet release as autumn leaves separate from caring branches.

November winds tempered by November rains dampen
Their graceful flight as clumsily now, habits torn, they sink,
Defeated, like grieving women they flock, landing in a hush;
The park stands still, now a vanquished landscape, hues of brown,
Bare dark scraggy limbs outstretched begging for alms;
Its trees, battalion like, have now but all surrendered their arms.

They stand resigned and obedient to their tamer, a prelude to
Seasonal suffering as the hands of mistress winter.
With the vengeance of a woman scorned, she unleashes howling winds;
Broken limbs lie scattered on the sodden earth whilst fluffy snow
Offers a futile dressing; still angry tempests and cruel winds hurl
Tree trunks onto the ground; a sudden frenzy of the untamed shrew

And there I stand in wonder of it all, at that which time dictates,
As I watch the unending newness of change.

Domes of Jerusalem

Golden domes that crown the noblest of cities,
May the rosy morning greet you,
And the violet of the evening bid you farewell;
How shall I call you?
Hallelujah of the stones.

Songs compiled in the skies of my Jerusalem,
Garlands of victory, refreshed by heaven's dew;
Do you watch over the children of Palestine, and
Together with the walls that surround the City
Console the bereaved mothers?

Domes that bend over love,
Around you circles the dove.
The young leaves on tree-tops caress you,
The stars converse with your ancient
Walls, your reminiscence of the past.

I sigh as I remember you in my journey,
Remembering my joy when my eyes
First saw you on my pilgrimage,
Longing to enter the City gates
You greeted me with garlands of light.

A symphony to civilisation, the incarnation of prayers,
The enlightenment of the Sufis, the liberation of the soul;
Was this last winter harsh on you and your people?
A trivial question to a city destined
To be dedicated to worship.

For what is the harshness of winter compared
to the cruelty of man?
A whole people have been crucified
On the cross overshadowing your roofs,
On a Golgotha where onlookers have long gone.
Roman centurions, too, have left this eerie spot.
Only lamentations of Mary Magdalene reverberate still.

Flakes are shed from your weary red stones,
Whilst the hushed whispers of the conifers
Conspire with the breeze as it dabs and dries
The tears of lament; the tears of the Domes
Consoled by the toll of a bell, and the call of a minaret.

Dolls

The scent of history lingers around two forlorn dolls,
Miniatures dressed in velvet, now frayed and well worn;
One in a dark red frock, the hem set off with fur,
The other dressed all in blue, with matching cap and shoes.
Flowers from a bygone autumn, dried, neatly pressed lie
Hemmed in between; the teddy bear grins, unconcerned,
Content, his rounded face matching his tum.
Toyland's philosopher declares: 'Good things come to an end.'

Glassy eyes staring back conceal play secrets of old,
Transporting wistful onlookers to a bygone world of fuzzy
Remnants of memories, in sound and vision, of daughters two.
Mother escapes to the living room, photographs of loved ones,
Clustered on the polished sideboard; bright laughing eyes
Sparkle, for an instant, for; memories unfold only to retreat.
Seasons, rolling waves in time and space, they come and go;
Only seasoned trees, old-timers, nod and wave in understanding.

The evening discreetly bows out and retreats;
The sun draws blue velvet curtains and falls into bed;
Nothing is left now but the vestibules and niches of the night,
Where thoughts roam, soaring over sky-scraping cities,
Seeking daughters by the shores of icy seas, far and forbidden,
To return them to their place in the sun. Reunited with dolls,
Musty smells of old may rekindle carefree childhood times,
And the murmur of swaying trees paint landscapes of the past.

Memories

In my heart dwells love and longing;
Anxiety is a shadow that haunts my days and nights.

Images of the past come to my aid:
I hear the children's laughter sound tinkling bells,
Their school certificates and copy books
Stare back at me with painful innocence;
Pink curtains with flowered prints in my daughters' room
Flutter, caressed by the evening breeze
In our home; in Jerusalem

In the garden, the basil, the jasmine,
The carnation, and the rose scent the air;
I recall such moments of peace and delight
In my country; in Palestine.
Palestine!

The very word, its tone, its resonance,
Make my heart yearn and memories flood back.
And in remembrance the heart finds solace.

Dunes

Dunes; the spring of the poet has dried up;
The oasis of flickering thoughts and images,
Word by word deconstructed and shrivelled;

Alone in a desert without a compass or guide
I stand, surrounded by muted golden sands,
As relentless winds sift and pile mile-high;

Self-imprisoned within their unending chain,
Wall after wall blocks my futile attempts to
Break through deceptive warm soft barriers;
Detached, unconcerned they keep guard.

Expectant of forceful hot winds to scatter
Their sands, I resign myself to meditate
The infinite horizons of this silent domain;

This now is my sole occupation, my sentence;
No dreams for the night, no goals for the day
The dream of poetry, a mirage, visits me no more.

For the stream of rhyme has been swallowed
By the fleeting sands of time immemorial,
Or is it a trickle and my anguish is the sign?

Ballad of the Rose

I looked at each rose and wondered,
Sad that such splendour
Does not transform time into joy,
But rather is passed by, unheeded
As from bud to bloom it withers away.

A rose stands brilliant
Like a temptress, petulant petals
Tinged with shades of pink.
Shaped so exquisite,
Its petals fold and kiss.

I rouse myself from this mesmeric trance, only
To stop by a rose tinged with the lilac of the
Blue moon that appears silently at eventide;
Such a rose surely belonged to my home.

Cut rose in hand, father stoops and
Quietly says, "Take it to your Grandfather";
In the spacious family home he lies, immobile
In a bed with bright brass polished posts;
Fair of complexion, hair now turned snow white,
A dignitary in his day, a pillar of the community
Revered by town folk for his good deeds
But now a prisoner of his own body.

With awe and in innocence I enter,
Small steps towards the frail figure.

I give him the rose and kiss the withered hand;
Saddened that in his garden he can never stand
Or caringly pick the scented rose himself,
He must wait – a seven-year-old
Brings nature's floral beauty to his side.
I kiss his hand, as is custom in my land; lest I forget
I am reminded by father's whispered words.

Human touch to the sick is heavenly comfort.
But did it make the old man happy or sad?
Nostalgic thoughts, a yearning for the past;
Perhaps a little wiser as he must have realised
How in our rush we miss the essence of life.
Thus, the rose bud, unnoticed, blossoms and fades;
Blithely we skip to drink the fragrance of blooms
As journeying through our brief lives we
Blindly squander golden opportunities.

I wake from my reverie in an English garden so
Thrilling in its freshness, exquisite in beauty. It holds me
Enchanted, rooted at this spot of nature's wonder
As the fragrant memory of a rose in my Palestine lingers.

Bird of grief

Bird of grief, strange bird
Did you visit me and yearn to stay?
Bird of grief, when will you fly,
Soar up to a star
Or do you want to make my heart your home?

The time has come for you to depart
Overseas, to explore the unknown;
Will you leave, beautiful one,
And allow the heart to rest?
Will you leave today
And allow the bird of paradise to alight,
A nightingale to sing the dreams of my youth?

In the Park

There is a park embraced by the mountains,
Visited by the late-comers of a summer's holiday,
Watched by majestic cedars, as setting sun floods
Past memories of civilizations ancient and proud.

Here I stand intoxicated with wonder;
Inexplicable is my joy,
Not related to love or youth
But a joy of sheer being
Beyond the limits of my own person,
Belonging to this union with nature.

Through the trees a wide open arch
I spy, but much too soon narrows to a close;
I watch as the sun gathers its beams
Before a final mellow orange curtain falls.

A lonely wind moans, lamenting summer's
Departure and the distant arrival of autumn,
As the last of the holidaymakers retreat;
The mountains re-embrace the park,
Whilst stout cedars stand attention,
Bracing themselves for the feisty winds of fall.

Baghdad

Worried and anxious is my heart as stone by stone
Baghdad is being dismantled, destroyed, and demolished;
For greed, pride, and ignorance have their sway as
Myopic eyes and long arms conspire, and aspire to acquire;
I love that city of long history, learning and mystery
Of dreams, of Shehrazad and the travels of Sindbad.

Domes glint in sunset, as graceful minarets soar high
Towards the blush dark sky, lit by a delicious crescent;
Orange blue stars shimmer and twinkle for attention;
Aladdin on his magic carpet scans the lands below.
His magic lamp seeks to rescue from a wizened wizard
A precious princess to rescue and to hold.

How relevant, how true today, as the search continues.
Our love, deep and consuming, wide and enduring, persists,
Until our princess of liberty is back to rekindle our days;
Do not bomb Baghdad, malign the magic, destroy the dream.
Baghdad the city of chivalry and beauty, born and bred,
Where damsels crafted dance, and craftsmen danced our future;
Poetry, music, and the works of the mind, competed in harmony;
You palmed away our Palestine; now the centre of our gravity.

Your carpet bombing is futile on a city that magic carpets weaves;
Do not bomb Baghdad for it is the land of Eden,
Of Sumerian legends and Noah and his Ark.
Hammurabi's laws were written here,
The Ten Commandments carved in stone.
Do not bomb Baghdad as history will not forgive you, nor will we.

The Pine Grove

Like sisters in a convent you congregate;
In subdued tones you converse while you sway;
Gentle is the movement, contentment is the mood;
I want to take refuge among you,
I want shelter from a world of shock and hurt.
You are in the world, but your serenity prevails.

Like disciplined sentinels you stand,
Watching the ever-changing canvas of the skies,
While the birds are busy homemaking
In your tender welcoming branches;
And when they sing, your motherly love overflows
With taught emotion as you clap and sway.

The birds have roosted, their heads lowered;
Evening approaches; the setting sun paints the sky
Violet, pink and fiery red.
Day is done. With the stars your vigil is kept.
Is this your treasured time of respite?
Dawn breaks; none but you is the wiser

The Giant

In my 'ghorba' as evening creeps up,
I am heavy, sunk in blue depths of sadness,
While twilight's silent shadows lengthen.
My soul, startled, takes flight to a lost seaside,
A bay aged by years and years of history's waves.

I am alone, at the mercy of a terrible giant;
It scoops me up onto a craggy peak while
Laughter echoes across the desolate range;
As the giant and his shadow rock and swagger;
My strangled voice dares to ask: "What is it you seek?"

"My meagre possessions are yours, as alas,
My soul has fled, not wanting to be possessed";
"The wealth I seek is not of this world," the giant mocks,
"'tis your memories I crave to own upon these rocks".
He leans forward, Goliath-like, and stares me in the eye.

Anxiety tempered by anger steels my trembling limbs;
"You will and can never posses my prized treasure;
My memories are my roots anchored true and deep;
My love, my companions, glimpses of my motherland,
The scent of orange blossom, the sight of fans of palm.

The flowers and shrubs that dot those holy hills
Betray the presence of the usurper who stole my homeland.
An innocent, unarmed youth confronts the aggressor.
So deep was his love for Palestine that he gave his life for it;
Such memories are what connect me to my motherland."

Nascent words in stature grew, as the ogre retreated out of view,
His mumbled echoes as if in pensive chant I heard:
"The scent of orange blossom, a youth confronts aggression,
The scent of orange blossom, a youth confronts aggression,
The scent of orange blossom, a youth confronts aggression."

The shadows on the landscape lengthened;
The mountains and valleys yawned, bored, old, so very old;
Bald peaks caught dazzling drizzling rays of sinking sun;
I retraced steps back to the city flooded by man-made lights;
Life's bustle at my window spied; my soul rooted in Palestine.

Canadian Awtumn

What words can colour your splendour,
Clad in royal gold and hues of amber;
Amazing is the inimitable russet treat,
Whilst competing blazing reds complete
Fiery torches illuminating a festive march,
A mélange of orange and gold in the brush.

There is celebration in the realm of trees;
With the advent of autumn. They seize
The sun with its streaming golden rays,
As baby clouds, ablaze
With tinged hems, peep to spy this dramatic
Extravaganza, unique in vast good Canada.

Yet with sadness this parade is met,
For it is not a welcoming event,
But a farewell party to the waving leaves
As branches caressed by gentle breeze,
Anticipating, brace for the wind's mischief play
Stripping boughs of their exotic display.

I survey the trees in my garden beau,
Deserted fragile nests hang from the boughs.
Stark nude branches, a crisp cold evening,
Bare arms plead for the bursting of spring;
I ponder this sad farewell to the leaves tonight,
Parallels to man's live drama,exit stage right.

Lament

Not for Gaza, but loss of humanity in humanity
For those massacring your children and your old
Degraded the human and lauded the humanoid
No light in their eyes; their conscience is dead
And the women of Gaza cannot be consoled
For their children are no more

The city on the crossroads of centuries past charms
Arms open to traders; now criss-crossed with arms
Caravans of old that threaded and trudged the Sinai
Carried spices, gold, and silks from so far away China
Makes way for modernity; marvel now at the 'Merkava'!
Flattening your citrus orchards; bellowing fire and lava

From land and sea your peoples came and settled
Sufis and men of faith found welcome at your shores
The palm trees reached out to dome and minaret
Christian and Muslim men lived in perfect harmony
Now the children of Israel to seek your children come
Showers of phosphorous lights that come and come

Pharaoh, Alexander, and Napoleon conspired to subdue
Allenby and a letter from Balfour schemed a ruse for you
Laid claim on behalf of those who claimed were 'chosen'
Chosen by who, chosen for what, chosen why? And why
Did those blind in their heart invest trust in legend and folklore?
The blind are now both deaf and dumb; your children forlorn

How fearful is the hate behind such weapons that trigger
How sad that neighbour and spectator do not lift a finger
A sound is heard in Gaza; the sound of bitter acid weeping
For the mothers of Gaza are crying blood for their children
They refuse to be comforted; their grief acute yet well hidden
Media pumps sound and vision; yet only pain for the bedridden

From dark velvet skies baubles of golden colour burst to grace
Your skyline trailing white tails float seductively to colour your face
Come children of Gaza tis Season's gifts from the children of Israel
Phosphorous burns to the screams; not of delight but of living hell
Those blind in their heart invested trust in legend and folklore
The blind are now both deaf and dumb; your children forlorn

You birthed 'intifada' from land's living stones and stood rock solid
While presidents, rulers, and the like, debated words and plotted
Your million and a half fenced in; besieged, tagged living exhibits lie
Stripped sliced and cut off are you from your dear mother Palestine
As in time past Gaza you were laid waste and plundered in vain
Yet your living stones are made to reinvent and spring to live again.

The Messenger

Sudden exhilaration gushed springs of joy,
As reflection, my comfort and fleeting companion
On my homeward journey, awoke
Childhood images of olive trees, geraniums,
Whilst the anemone and the cyclamen stood,
Miniature candles where the feet of Jesus trod
And the winds of Galilee blew in a mystical dance.

But such blithe images were whisked away as
Depression like a cruel hag, crafty in ways of deception,
Sowed its seeds. Self-doubt, life's futility and
Depleted self-esteem questioned: why this suffering?

On a hill, a shepherd tending his flock came into view;
I watched; no words passed between us, as hallowed
Harmony prevailed; the scene and image faded away;
There was sunset, blessedness, peace;
Unexpected was the spring of joy that washed over me.

To A Day

Here you arrive on time's relentless express;
The sun has lifted the curtain of night
Ushering you in with a gorgeous dawn of colour;
And so I meet you!
With what shall I fill your precious irreplaceable space?
Hence I wonder about our being in the here and now;
Are we companions fulfilling a plan?
Are we a truth or a fantasy?

Passing travellers who met by chance
And have to be together, you and me;
For without you I would not have been;
I cannot bypass your journey,
I have to live you,
Live you in an ideal fashion;
As the only day I have and will ever know;
I shall pour into you the essence of my heart,
And crown you with an olive branch.

Listen! A chirping bird accompanies your march,
Like a melodist playing his joyous awakening,

While gracefully the boughs dance to the tune
And the olive tree that presses on my window,
Branches bowed, smiles with dignity;
I live the whole drama of your manifestation;
Thus we will be united as a particle of a truth.

More awful than our conception
is the mystery of creation;
In its myriad facets you share in its mosaic.
The evening has started its quiet march;
The sun kisses the ocean bidding you farewell,
While waves embrace its golden fingers of light
As you gradually, quietly, yet bravely fade away;
A curtain will be drawn on your dramatic play
Today; does it mean you are gone for good,
Or are you etched in the sanctity of eternity?
Tomorrow you are certain not to be;
But in uncertainty, I may exist or not at all;
If I am still in the world of the living,
I shall keep your memory etched deep in my heart,
Crowned by the song of a bird in an olive tree.

Al-Hambra

In Hambra I stand, as centuries roll back a walkway,
A sense of déjà vu, as I step into the before and past;
The boundaries of dreams and history blurred;
The hands of change in memories entwined,
In wonderland amongst cascading arabesque
I wander; as calm and quiet comfort my turbulent soul

Turrets, towers, citadels, chambers, courts and minarets
Capture loitering visitors by marbled pillars and arch, pondering
Latticed windows, which shielded once damsels young and fair,
Giggling, whispering wishful naughty nothingness, and peeping to spy
Men of substance, serious in matters of state and fate
Bustling in and out of outer courts and chambers below.

A blink of wakefulness shakes my reverie, for
Gardens like no others are the Genaralif; perhaps, I muse,
The creation of a caliph, calculating and considerate as he
Pined the Damascene garden now faded, lost to his senses
Where jasmine, myrtle, carnation and rose bush grew,
Reconceived from imagination on foreign soil.

The rose, pride of Damascus, its intoxicating scent transported
Images of fountained courtyards, whilst in every home
Its people reclined, content amidst azure mosaics.
Though great was this Caliph's renown, yet wretched was he too.
He eased his longing for home in sister-like whispers
To a solitary palm tree on an Andalusian plane.

The fountains, the orangeries, the cypress trees, and laurels,
Decked arches supported by slender pillars to a bygone world
My mind drifts back to them, fleeing the glare and greed of this age.
The wooded grounds, hushed in silence, await the crowd's departure.
Al-Hambra! You enfold yourself in the arms of your solitude,
Embraced by of the wind; conquered but proud, haughty yet sad.

Resentful at the folly of those who surrendered you to posterity,
Strains from Andalusian lute and flute tease your silence no more;
Even the heady scent of jasmine and basil is spent,
Amongst the streams and flower beds of this dreamland,
Alhambra! An unsettled spirit roams your wooded grounds;
A melancholy pervades as evening solemnly descends.

Modernity cannot comfort your soul or shake your distant memories;
In your estrangement the snow-capped Nevada range looks on.
Ancient, tall companion cypress trees enshrine and comfort you;
In the hush of the night the sailor moon lingers over your ruins,
Pulling ebb-like, to carry you away from your unending misery,
Whilst midnight spreads its blue veil, shrouding your eternal mystery.

Our Garden

Peace and harmony cohabitate in our garden;
Dark green are the leaves of the olive tree,
Its tops fluttering silvery flags signal to
The apples tinged with gold, whilst some
With blushing cheeks are turning red;
The languid vine rests on old wooden poles,
Translucent bunches nestle amongst caring leaves,
Whilst the flaming red flowers of the pomegranate lure
The almond's blossom, virgins in bridal attire flutter and fall;
Like lit candles, the orange's florets exude intoxicating scent;
The birds, welcome guests, prepare intricate clusters of nests.

Friends from my youth, come to our garden;
Let us with merriment enjoy nature's playground,
For such times fade as the years play catch-up;
Come, let the scent of the roses tease our memories,
As we watch twitching birds act nature's drama;
We shall hide behind the trunks of the wise olive trees,
And in the heavily laden orange grove we shall frolic.

But do not bring love's troubles to our verdant patch,
Do not even mention the word in whisper or in jest,
For the pains of love are but a thorn in youthful hearts,
Making them bleed and filling them with anxious thoughts;
But let's come together that we might spite and mock Cupid;
Fear him not for he does not have us in his sights; yet

I beg you not to come if love's arrows are stuck in your hearts,
Ones that make your hearts bleed and your sleep perturbed;
Pinch rose buds from your cheeks, sprinkle stars in your eyes,
For then our garden will become a pilgrimage for memories;
Its walkways of calm and beauty becoming jagged paths of pain.

The olive moans in your ear laments of sorrow and yearning,
Whilst the fruit of the vine's delirious desires torment you
And your petulant lips are set aflame by the apple's blush.
Pomegranate florets with burning hearts brand you,
And the bees and the butterflies become false messengers;
The nightingale's song uncups a well of tears.

I shall look for you and find you pining under the orange trees;
Fragrant intoxicants compel you to solitude and hopeless dreams;
It is an imperative not to allow love into our garden.

Come only for fun and laughter, and to make merry
Or else I shall close the garden gate to all those smitten.
For once love enters, who can chase it away?
Once memories nestle in its bowers and sully its scents,
Who can extract it from its floral carpet or foliaged branches?
Come and make merry with hearts free of every bond,
But not to pine and dwell on torturous memories.
For our garden is where peace, beauty and purity abide.

My City

You are my city; yet from it I am banished;
As at its gates I stand, exiled and bewildered,
A passerby intrudes and asks: "What is this city to you?"
It is my Truth; I wish they all knew this.
What remains of me is brokenness;
The wounds I cherish, they are mine,
As I commit myself to their searing pain.

Aimlessly I roam its desert, but compelled
I keep looking back to glimpse its walls and towers;
Joy overcomes me; hopeless, limitless, unfounded,
Now that I measure how little I have travelled
From my City; from my Truth.
Though tempted I avoid the lush green oasis;
Though thirsty I do not stop to drink from its limpid pools.

Nothing excites me as I wander without purpose.
The desert of my sorrows is my constant companion,
As I retrace my steps, drawn back to its walls, and
In the twilight I now spy my City tinged with gold;
Its twinkling lights a sprinkling of stars in the sunset;
And as the sun rises, I still stand at its gates in exile.

Here, I see the tops of its trees hanging over its walls,
Throwing their shade beyond its interior,
Reaching out to expel the relentless sun.
How I long to sit in their shade;
Will my love appear at its gate?

If only once I will be the seer,
Undeserved rewards will be my gain;
Will such dreams ever come true,
Or must memories be my sole companion?
Days fade away, fleeting memories die,
Only my love of the City remains.

A wanderer comes upon me, a dweller of my City, and
Talks of the domes and spires that garnish its beauty;
Hauntingly beautiful and enchanting are his wistful words.
He departs, illuminating my thoughts with joyful ecstasy,
And I wonder if my momentary happiness was due to the
Memories stirred by this encounter; or if it was the dweller
Personifying the City that made me yearn to return.

And when the winds rustle in the boughs of its trees,
My City, vivid, transcends all human desire,
A gentle sweet sadness blows through my being,
And my heart again craves for visions of my City.
At a certain hour of twilight, my soul will light up,
Inflamed by that dancing fire
Which is the City dwelling in me still,
And I will return there, an exile no more.

A Continent Called Palestine

The rounded hills of Palestine
Oblivious are of the secrets dormant within
So are the baby grasses that sway on the 'tal'
Caressed by the breezes of an early spring
Tender innocent daughters of our present time
Ignorant of eras past lying deep in its recesses
Of Canaanites in citadels and temples to Ashira
To you psalms of praise echo and roofs rise

Philistines their cities shoring the shores of Palestine
The Hebrews' kingdom one of many but not alone
Forgotten are the roads and city squares that lie beneath
The clamour of fighters has in its earth long receded
Forgotten are the athlete charioteers furiously chasing
To win the glory of the city and the love of a pretty maiden
From fallen idols, domes, minarets, and synagogue rose
So you can become the pilgrims respite for a thirsty spirit

In ambition, jealousy and unrequited love, your human
Tenants toiled and then spoilt your fields dear Palestine
No one can claim you except those who sacrificed to love you
In ordeal and glory, in lush spring and harsh winter clung
To your bosom; now as did our ancestor we people of Palestine
Offer the love of blood and sweat to mix in and enrich your soil.